ECLIPSE

poems by

Sarah Wolbach

Finishing Line Press
Georgetown, Kentucky

ECLIPSE

ACKNOWLEDGMENTS

Grateful acknowledgment is made to the editors of the following
publications where these poems, some of which have been subsequently
revised, originally appeared:

Birds Piled Loosely: "Earth and Sky"
Bristlecone: "Anniversary Hike," "Killing Time," "Wild"
Comstock Review: "Erased"
Dos Gatos Press: "Home"
Fixed and Free Anthology, 2021: "Power," "The Holidays after You,"
"Why You Asked Me to Scatter Your Ashes in the Walmart Parking Lot"
Malpaís Review: "Open Heart" (original title: "Who You Are")
Snakeskin: "Daily"
Taos Journal of Poetry: "Whale Fall"
Wild Roof Journal: "Cyclone"

Publisher: Leah Huete de Maines
Editor: Christen Kincaid
Cover Art: Andrea Stöckel, CC0 1.0 UNIVERSAL
Author Photo: Ginger Legato
Cover Design: Elizabeth Maines McCleavy

Order online: www.finishinglinepress.com
also available on amazon.com

Author inquiries and mail orders:
Finishing Line Press
PO Box 1626
Georgetown, Kentucky 40324
USA

Contents

for Roy

Partial Eclipse, 8/21/17

As clouds obscure the diminishing
sun, you join me outside.
You have been reading *Hamlet*
and want to talk about the father's ghost.
Why did he appear first
to Hamlet's friends, not to his son?
Why not dive into the murder?
Why meander?

You have worn out your wonder
with me, forever digging shallow
plots. *Suspense*, I say.
Delay feeds the madness.
Murder, mother, drowning, poisoned blade.
All die. It takes time.

How can I receive this offering of eclipse?
Your voice clutters the silence.
There are shades of dim worth pondering,
like the gloom before rain when we turn on the lamp.
Today I await the sublime, the intersection
of galactic and particular, but you will not stop
talking, wandering through Hamlet's haze,
the ramparts, despair. I should leave you,
vanish indoors, pretend dim into dark,
chant as the earth is un-tethered. But I stay.

The moon shifts to the other side of the sun.
Light crescendos into the long afternoon,
and the ghost slips away.

Open Heart

The night before they sliced open your heart
and replaced the aortic valve while you lay
cold and dead under hot lights

they brought your roommate a meal
wrapped in antiseptic plastic, impossible
to eat. You slid from your bed and helped him.

You slit the plastic sleeve of utensils, placed
a spoon in his hand. You tore the aluminum lid
from a lump of chocolate pudding.

You unwrapped a soggy sandwich,
gray beef with a scrap of lettuce
light years from the light it drank

to become itself. Weeks later,
we drove past a ragged man
holding his sign upside down,

drooping at the curb. You said *food*,
so we pulled into the drive-through lane
of KFC, bought a bucket of fried chicken

and a Coke. We went back. You said,
Here, partner and he said, *Thank you,
God.* So many kindnesses.

Stray dogs you rescued with a leash and collar
you made from your belt. The winter coat
you left on a park bench. Money for anyone

who asked. You thanked veterans for their service,
shook hands with drifters, the rudderless,
embraced locked hearts without keys.

Our First Emergency

The day we went snorkeling
in the Sea of Cortez,
my mask leaked a little.
We pulled hand over hand
in shallow water through the cove,
over smooth stones a few yards
from the shore. Tentative
but determined, I followed you.

Perhaps in another life I drowned.
I have always been afraid
to submerge my face under water.
Just breathe, you said.

For the first time, I breathed
under water. I peered beneath
the thin surface of the ocean.
Through silt and broken shells,
a round, thorny creature with teeth
scuttled under my shadow,
unspooling a striped sea snake.
Blue and yellow fish shimmered
in electric light.

Then you touched a hovering
stingray. It stung your hand.
Tearing off your mask, crying out in pain,
you splashed toward the shore.
I knew we had to get help immediately,
find a balm for your swelling hand.

Why don't you go—I'll stay awhile,
I wanted to say. Instead, I waded back
to shore. I placed the sea and its colors
in the back of my mind, on a small shelf
that over time became very crowded.

Why You Asked Me to Scatter Your Ashes in the Walmart Parking Lot

After you could no longer drive and before you succumbed
to a wheelchair, you heard that some stores had electric carts.
One morning we went shopping at Walmart.
Shrugging off my help, you stumbled with your cane
through the automatic doors.

A friendly greeter found you a cart.
You enjoyed a stale cookie and a very bad cup of coffee at Subway.
You cruised around the store,
    smiled at every customer and child and stock clerk and cashier
    examined clothing shoes vitamins electronics tools food toys
        cosmetics
    tried on hats and watches
    hid dollar bills behind cereal boxes
    said *Buenos días* to a family speaking Spanish.

You motored into the wheelchair customer line,
paid for your underwear, a bottle of shampoo, a box of raisins,
    a package of disposable razors.
The cashier looked you in the eyes and smiled,
said, *Have a nice day, sir.*

In the parking lot, I helped you into the car, buckled your seatbelt.
You told me about the world that didn't include me.
I can't wait to do it again, you said.

Daily

There are roof dogs in San Miguel
whose feet never touch the earth.

I walked past them every day, navigating
slick cobblestones to the café where we met

to eat fly-kissed guacamole and greasy
tortilla chips, sip Coca-Cola from warm bottles.

In the street, vendors hawked peanuts and roses.
A boy with a twisted foot and dim eyes

slumped on the curb outside the café
next to a stack of newspapers, glowering

at anyone who looked his way. We wondered
who looked after him. Every day we put

pesos in his cup, took a newspaper
to read to each other in bed.

Sometimes you bought me roses
with tiny thorns.

Slayer, San Miguel de Allende

In the market, women scrape thorns
from prickly pears, stack the green pads.
On his mother's lap, a boy nibbles a tortilla,
eyes a starving dog slinking past the butchers
sharpening their knives.

They sell chicken feet, cow feet, pig knuckles,
heads of pigs / lambs / goats / calves,
slices of *arrachera* from the belly of a steer,
tripe from the stomach of a cow.
They weigh livers, hearts, and brains for soup.

We often eat lunch at the market:
albondigas with *frijoles*, stewed *nopales*—
slices of prickly pear boiled with salt.
A smiling woman fills our plates. A sullen boy
brings bottles of warm Coca-Cola.

One afternoon, we walk in the hills beyond town,
as usual talking about lunch, your indifferent sons,
our dog waiting for us at home. We find
yellow blossoms of prickly pear, peppercorns
strewn beneath a tree, the ruins of a house.

We stumble onto the body of a ragged white pup
hanging by its back legs from a low branch of mesquite.
Broken ribs poke through mangy fur.
Talking of boys and dogs, and out of nowhere,
it seems, we are talking about butchery.

Power

Your last winter, before the seizures
and strokes, you motored in your power chair
to the Senior Center for lunch every day.
You didn't want me to drive you.
It was a wobbly ride on a narrow sidewalk
along busy St. Francis Drive, then another
mile on a crumbly street
of potholes and weeds. Snarling
dogs behind shabby fences.

You sat with Bixby, Pat, and Juanita
at the Lunch Bunch table;
ate Sloppy Joes, chicken fingers,
fish on Fridays, and pudding;
drank milk from child-sized cartons.
Bixby's son lived in Brazil.
Pat's apartment was like a jail cell.
Juanita was ravenous.

One day at noon, a sudden snow spilled
like crystallized foam from the sky,
disappearing the world.
I went to find you. I found you
plugging along the vanishing
street, buffeted by sleet,
your wheels slick with ice.
I asked you to get in the car.
You refused. *I will not.*
I insisted. *You must.*
You gripped the joystick
with your wet glove, would not let go.

I didn't love you anymore.
I drove home, shivering with fury,
not knowing if today's emergency
would be the last. Ten minutes later,
you slid down the driveway
and through the door, nearly tipping over.
You blew warm breath onto your cold hands.
Smiling as you brushed snow from your coat, you said,
I'm not dead yet.

Waiting Room of the VA Hospital

We waited for hours. We watched
a movie on a massive screen.

Bad guys held down another bad guy,
stuffed a live snake into his mouth.

After a few moments, the tail stopped
waving. I opened a tattered copy

of *National Geographic.* I read
that a young male lion, taking over

a pride after killing the patriarch, kills
the cubs. After tossing them aside

he grabs a lioness by the nape of
her neck, hot fur thrilling

in his mouth as he perfectly, necessarily,
rapes her, forcing more cubs.

We drove home during rush hour,
stopped at Denny's on the way.

You ordered the Grand Slam, eggs over easy.
I ordered a green chile cheeseburger with fries.

We joked about deserving comfort food
after our long wait in that ferocious room.

Feral creatures lurked under the table.

Newlyweds

Let's have a parade!
   we'd shout; then we marched
      around our cluttered apartment
      in Queens,

you in front with a battered trumpet,
   me behind you wearing
      a necklace of donkey teeth
      from Mexico.

We wore the funny hats
   you bought in Union Square—
      yours a jester's cap with bells,
      mine a floppy hobo's hat.

You tooted on the trumpet,
   and I belted out a wordless song.
      We giggled and marched
      from room to room with Scamper

leaping and barking around us,
   jumping onto and off the bed,
      laughing like children—
      and we were.

Erased

That night at the Zipper Theater in New York
we saw a forgettable play with a slamming
screen door, a vintage car fender, and at least
one naked girl. Afterwards, we clapped, we gathered
our things and ourselves, then the woman behind you
stood and swept her black cape over her shoulders,
the bottom of it covering your face for a moment,
blinding you. Nothing like that happened again.
Not after the play about a woman who falls in love with a goat
or *The Tempest* with a three-headed Ariel.
Not after the flamenco show at Carnegie Hall
or the showcase where a tango dancer's shoe flew off
mid-syncopation, and she kept dancing.
Not after the play where the characters mumbled in bed,
as we do, and the house lights, never turned down,
shone into our laps for hours.

Earth and Sky

Before we had Scamper put down that morning,
I begged you to go outside and find
a few sticks or a handful of dirt,
bring them indoors so she could smell
the essential earth before dying.
You humored me.
Because the elevator was broken, you walked
six stories down to the filthy street,
found a few sticks, brought them up.

Years later, at the Bandelier ruins in New Mexico,
you climbed a series of five ladders
to the Alcove House, 140 feet above the pines.
You have forgotten your eager grasp
of the splintering rungs as you climbed
into the cliff dwellings of the ancients
and the frightening descent, when you hugged
the ladders so hard you bruised your ribs.

Stories of kindness and courage mean nothing to you now.
I have given up trying to remind you.
You do remember Scamper, your dream-come-true dog,
how she curled at your feet, how she licked your face.

September 13th, 2001

It was raining. Our dirty clothes had piled up.
I washed them in the laundry room on the first floor.
Our apartment building and the streets were silent.

Handing me the plastic bag of chow mein
and Kung Pao chicken, the Chinese delivery man
traced tears down his cheeks with his fingers,
pointed to the rain outside then west to the smoldering
ruins. Yes, I said. Yes.

After 9/11, some people shut down. Others chose to live.
It's a strange turn of the heart, isn't it, whether to limp
into the abyss or turn away? The doused ashes
and the fallen were all we thought about,
talked about, despaired to comprehend.

We unwrapped the chopsticks, scraped the ends
so there would be no splinters, then devoured the food.
The next morning, we turned on the news.
Foul-smelling smoke crept along the horizon.
You scrambled some eggs. It was still raining.

Traditions

At Thanksgiving dinner, my cousins and I stuck
pitted black olives on our fingers and waggled them
at the grownups, then fingered with impunity
sweet gherkins from the same dish, licked butter
from soft, sweet rolls, smeared gravy on our clothes
when they weren't looking.
The phone always rang during pie—the aunties—
long distance so expensive in the Stone Age, and
Everyone Here talked to Everyone There.
Then the grownups drank homemade wine.

We spent our first Thanksgiving together
in your dirt-cheap casita, in a small town
by the Sea of Cortez, a block from a beach
strewn with pebbles and pelican bones. I flew
from León that morning, sashayed down the stairs
from plane to tarmac, hair tangled in the wind.
I expected a feast. At least a plan, a ta-da!
But the kitchen counter held only a box of Cheerios,
a loaf of bread, a jar of peanut butter, a package of *Pinguinos*—
all the local bodega supplied.

Cheerios and peanut butter are still your favorite foods.
This year, I stock up on gherkins and olives.
I buy sliced turkey by the pound, boxed gravy
and Stove Top stuffing, a pumpkin pie baked last week,
and canned whipped cream—such fun to squirt at you,
waggling my black-olived fingers at you,
breaking bread with you in our little house
over the river and through the woods.

Anniversary Hike

Lost in the woods after missing the sign
with a curving arrow advising us of the trail,
we wander for hours unthreaded
from the needle of direction.

I grip a sharp stone in my right hand,
binoculars in my left. I will break a skull
if I have to—of a mountain lion, most likely,
for we find paw prints in patches of November snow.

Sometimes we fathom how vulnerable we are
among the indifferent atoms of living things
and dead things. I set love aside for survival,
follow you cautiously into the forest's maw.

The light dims, becomes shadow-light.
The particles of the intimate boundary
between light and dark separate,
and in a split second the forest disappears,

becomes dark as a cavern after the candle
is snuffed out. Eyes useless, feet lost
underneath us. We hold cold hands, pull
in different directions. The forest growls.

Home

Every week, we bought firewood from an old man and his
twisted twig of a son, the wood cut from shrinking forests
in an ever widening desert around San Miguel, stacked high
on a tormented burro. In the remains of a Mexican hacienda
we found generations of dust. Ruins everywhere we looked:
in the faces of the old man and his son, in Mayan temples
in the Yucatán, in abandoned silver mines near Guanajuato,
in crumbling adobe dwellings in New Mexico, in derelict
tenements of the Lower East Side. Fascinated by the echoes
of disaster, we peered into wreckage, imagined it as our own.
We moved often, from city to city, each move a harbinger
of the ruin you would become over time, a disintegrating
temple, a sinkhole of blood. In Santa Fe, gas exploded in
the basement of our new house, cracking open the corner
of your studio. Broken glass sprayed into the street and
mingled with the soil in the garden. The wreck upended us.
We found a new house, but your heart wasn't in it, and a
pinched nerve eventually forced you into a wheelchair. No
more clambering up ladders, as you once did in the ruins of
Bandelier, climbing 140 feet into the ancient cliff dwellings of
the Anasazi. *While I still can,* you said.

Killing Time

I choose a bad restaurant for no good reason.
The *huevos rancheros* are greasy eggs
and stale tortillas smothered in lukewarm red chile.
The coffee is hot, brown water in a chipped cup.
At the next table sits a family of three—
two teenage parents and a baby they pass
back and forth across the table
along with a cell phone and a salt shaker.

While you lay dying in my arms, I murmured
"love is everything" over and over. What a strange
thing to say. I wish I had said only "I love you"—
less complicated. It was an interminable day
of bad choices. With each flavorless bite, I try
to forgive myself a little, love you more.

Threshold

I stumble over shadows.
Thresholds meander,
each door a perplexity.

I forgot about the final threshold.
I forgot that the dying lose
their hearing last of all.

I meant to say, "Good night, sweet prince."
I meant to play Satie's *Gymnopédies*,
as you had once requested.
But during the frantic chaos of your dying,
the last thing you heard
was the loud voice of the hospice nurse
telling me your temperature was 103^{0}
and your lungs were making a crackling sound,
and the paramedic saying,
Ma'am, I'm very sorry.

So furious you must have been.

Touching You

I drive through Wolf Creek Pass at dusk.
Hairpin turns, moon rising,
a shadow stalking across the road
littered with carcasses of deer,
smashed rabbits, and mice.
A dead coyote. A bloody skunk
hunkers down into its stink.
The dead are everywhere.

I fled the house where you died
in agony. I watched as your blood
drained from veins and capillaries,
pallor mortis turning your skin
to marble, a curtain falling
onto your empty stage.

For the last time, I touched your body,
cupped your hollow face in my hands,
smoothed your jaw, rested my palm
on your chest, hairless and concave
as always, now hopeless
without your beating heart.
Surprised, I discovered your navel
was perfectly round with straight sides.
For the first time, my finger dipped
into that smooth crater.

I confess my indifference,
that for 22 years I neglected to probe
every fissure and crevice
of your flesh the way lovers burrow
into stone, risking the smother
of avalanche, the silence of ice.

Tonight I drive through craters
and valleys, past the broken,
the dead, latticed in bone and shatter.

Trash

I should return your childhood to the trash:
the photos your mother took of you
wearing a cowboy hat, brandishing
your six-guns, decorating the Christmas tree.
Report cards, Mother's Day cards,
a lock of hair she snipped from your head
when you were two years old.

You threw the scrapbook away. By accident
I found it before the garbage truck came.
I tucked it into a drawer, thinking
that someday you might regret the impulse
and I could mend your lost childhood.
I preserve scraps of your life, remembering
the stories you told over and over:

your mother
        stabbing your father with a fork at the dinner table
          cheating on him with your 7th grade math teacher—
              you were the look out
        making you her little best friend, her inept advisor

your father   beating her beating her beating her
               shooting at you for fun with the deer rifle
                  he used years later to shoot himself
               disowning you for spite

It was too much responsibility, being the last voice
you heard. As you lay dying, unable to speak,
I cast through my dull, tired mind for people
who loved you. There weren't many.
"Your mother loved you," I said.
You shook your head.

I knew nothing. I should have left
your misery in the trash.

The Holidays After You

Swinging
on monkey bars
through Christmas week,
dangling
from the frame
of each date
on the calendar—
the festive and the ho-ho—if
I fall
I'll have to start over,
back up   trudge back
to the solstice   too dark
to calculate the hours and distance
required.
        Perpetual cusp
of winter, mine
to abide.

My grasp is weak.
Where is the thrust?
Where is the sway?

My hips accept
the invitation of gravity—
a new year forever
out of reach.

Cyclone

What are cyclones called when they stand still?
—*Pablo Neruda*

No name for existence after it ceases
to matter, to *be* matter.
Like you. Impossible
to pin down that butterfly
thrashing in the wind,
a mirage of wings.

After whirl and water,
there is nowhere to be.
The land has been scoured,
swept to sea, and the wind
is still. In a dream,

I heard your voice calling my name.
I think it was a dream.
I was afraid to get out of bed,
follow your vanishing voice
down that hallway.

I wish this merciless grief
were spent, dissipated,
allowing another storm
to blow itself into being.

But it rages, unrelenting.

Whale Fall

I thought I was done with you
until I heard the story of Tahlequah,
the orca whale whose silky calf

lived only a few hours after its birth.
Tahlequah balanced the corpse
on her forehead and her back,

kept it from sinking, and pushed it
for seventeen days and one thousand miles
through Puget Sound and the open sea.

She lifted the body as it sank—
hundreds of times—hoisting it
out of the water to take a breath.

When at last she released her calf, the carcass
sank to the sea floor—whale fall—
fare for scavengers in the dark.

I have carried my grief as Tahlequah
carried her dead calf, determined
not to let go. Pushing it to the surface

when it drops down. When
will I let it fall? Where might it settle?
My sea floor is a blanket of sand,

smooth and abiding.
What creatures in my darkness
might flourish with the gift of release?

Instead

After the burning, the mortuary assistant called.
Your husband has been returned to us.
This morning, he handed me a white cardboard box.

It is our anniversary. I should scatter your ashes,
recycle the box, write a love poem or a confessional, perhaps
one of each. Instead, I put on your paint-stained

orange sweatshirt and dirty orange cap,
your pink and orange and yellow sneakers—
tight and uncomfortable, not a problem for you

since you couldn't walk. No ceremony today.
I go to Walmart, your favorite store,
do what you would do on this cold day:

buy warm things for the men at St. Elizabeth's Shelter.
Every year you brought them sweaters and coats,
worried about them on cold nights.

I load the shopping cart with underwear,
sleeping bags, tarps, gloves, toothbrushes, socks.
The aisles are crowded with chattering

families, discounted merchandise. I pay,
then push the heavy cart to the car, limping
in your tight and uncomfortable shoes.

I stuff my purchases into the trunk.
You asked me once to scatter your ashes
in the Walmart parking lot. You were like that.

I will tomorrow. Perhaps I will.

Farewell

The evening news wraps up with a human
interest story. An old man and old woman
are pushed toward each other across the patio
in front of the Casa Real nursing home.
After a year apart, they embrace awkwardly
in their wheelchairs, murmuring and masked.

The camera moves closer.
We hear the faint tremble of the woman's voice—
Oh I love you I love you I love you—
the *Oh* at a higher pitch, then the pause, then the lilt of grief,
despair, rough, cold sheets, the terror of dying alone,
night after night, hundreds of nights, surrounded
by dying strangers, the strangling sound
as their breath, lung by lung, was torn away.
All I wanted was to hold you in a soft, cool bed.

You wore a mask. I wore a mask.
So did the paramedics who lifted you from the floor,
the aides who dripped morphine into your mouth,
the hospice nurse who pronounced you dead,
the mortician who zipped you into a red brocade body bag
        and wheeled you out the door.

I won't push your chair any more.
I will mingle rose petals with your ashes.
I will hold your mask to my mouth,
        breathe your last breath.
I will dream of your soft ocean eyes.
I will imagine a good life for you, a good death,
        and time will roll you away.

The Way We Did Things

Nine months after your death
I scramble three eggs,

soft and fluffy with a sprinkling of cheese,
the way you liked them.

I pour skim milk into your favorite
green plastic glass, half full,

place your special fork
on a folded square of paper towel.

I sit in your chair, scatter
Mrs. Dash onto the eggs

the way you used to,
from high above the plate,

stray particles falling
on the table you bought

years ago at Goodwill
for fifty dollars.

After breakfast, I wash
your plate and fork, then carry

our chairs outside. We listen
as a robin and a chainsaw

take turns making music.
We share a cup of coffee,

turning the handle
when we pass the cup.

We talk about Mexico: roses and marigolds,
huevos revueltos, our wedding

and the judge who married us—Dr. Vargas,
who also happened to be a dentist.

We spent our honeymoon with our dog
in a straw bale house

lent to us by friends, along with their car:
a VW Bug with a hole in the floor.

Scamper dug up the flowers in our friends' garden.
We scattered rose petals on the marriage bed.

There will be time, enough
to clear the table, to wash the cup.

Holding your soft hand,
I open the door, and return.

Wild

We used to say we'd hike
    up Bear Canyon to Atalaya,
       have a picnic.

Now I hesitate
    to step from flat
       to slant   to crumble

and you are gone.
    In my youth,
       in my seven-league boots,

I leapt from boulder
    to boulder
       over slits and chasms,

over gaping mouths
    of caves. I lit
       fires with my boots.

I walked over water
    on needle-thin planks. I fell
       but did not break.

I dwindled
    with you, meandered
       too long

in the flats. You stumbled,
    you broke, you fell
       into shatter. Now

you lie in the sand,
    old man, old glass
       changing color.

My nerves shiver
    the fall, the slant
        of shale.

Why not avalanche,
    scrape flesh to the bone?
        Why not

slip from a bridge
    and see where I land?
        I might skip

across water, might sink
    into sand. But if
        I must drown, why not

drown happy? I plan to be wild:
    Up-fall into darkness,
        become a bright stone.

With Thanks

I am grateful for the mentors, friends, and family members who supported me as I gathered earlier poems and wrote new ones for this collection. Lise Goett, who organized the manuscript, challenged me to be daring and resolute. Fellow poets Deanna Einspahr, Jean Fogel, Ginger Legato, Zoe Robles, Mary Morris, Kate O'Neill, and Emily Pepin provided insights and encouragement when the well was dry; and dear friends Jenna Ritter, Marie Gee, Dawn Wright, Laurie McGrath, Steve Reed, Carolyn Lamb, and Trish Wirtenson helped me find my feet in the darkness after Roy's death. Special thanks to Eileen Joyce for her wisdom and guidance, and to my mother, Judy Wolbach, who has always been my greatest champion.

Most of all, I am grateful for my dear husband, the love of my life. Roy, you were a true original: curious, creative, adventurous, playful, and kind. The world was a better place with you in it. Even when times were hard, you insisted on enjoying life. I am thankful for the richness of our life together—for ALL of it. I will miss you forever.

Sarah Wolbach grew up in Salt Lake City and attended San Francisco State University. After graduation, she was hired by W.W. Norton to promote and sell Norton's college textbooks in Texas. She settled down in Austin, where she became an independent contractor in the educational publishing field.

Sarah earned an MFA in poetry and playwriting from the Michener Center for Writers at UT Austin. With a postgraduate fellowship, she moved from Austin to San Miguel de Allende, Mexico, where she met and married Roy. They left Mexico for New York City, where they lived for several years. In 2008, they moved to Santa Fe, New Mexico.

After Roy's death in 2020, Sarah began to write and gather poems delving into their relationship, his death, and the aftermath. Many of those poems have been gathered into this collection.

Sarah's poems have appeared in many journals, including *Artful Dodge, Bristlecone, Comstock Review, Dos Gatos Press, Santa Fe Literary Review, Snakeskin, Taos Journal of Poetry, Wild Roof Journal,* and *Yalobusha Review.* She was a finalist for the 2023 Banyan Poetry Prize.

An avid birder and clarinet player, Sarah lives in Santa Fe with her dog, Joey.

www.ingramcontent.com/pod-product-compliance
Lightning Source LLC
Chambersburg PA
CBHW022052080426
42734CB00009B/1303